With a Twist of Rhyme

With a Twist of Rhyme

Over 200 Rhymes
Humorous, Folksy, Sarcastic
Plus One Hymn

Joann Sprangers Lee

AuthorHouse™ LLC
1663 Liberty Drive
Bloomington, IN 47403
www.authorhouse.com
Phone: 1-800-839-8640

© 2013 by Joann Sprangers Lee. All rights reserved.

No part of this book may be reproduced, stored in a retrieval system, or transmitted by any means without the written permission of the author.

Published by AuthorHouse   07/15/2013

ISBN: 978-1-4817-6281-6 (sc)
ISBN: 978-1-4817-6280-9 (hc)
ISBN: 978-1-4817-6279-3 (e)

Library of Congress Control Number: 2013910590

Any people depicted in stock imagery provided by Thinkstock are models, and such images are being used for illustrative purposes only.
Certain stock imagery © Thinkstock.

This book is printed on acid-free paper.

Because of the dynamic nature of the Internet, any web addresses or links contained in this book may have changed since publication and may no longer be valid. The views expressed in this work are solely those of the author and do not necessarily reflect the views of the publisher, and the publisher hereby disclaims any responsibility for them.

Author's Note

It's always been a pastime of mine—writing rhymes with a punch line or a little twist (hence the With a Twist of Rhyme). They were written as general observations or about family, friends and co-workers. I was born in the teeny Wisconsin town of Darboy (not on the map) and for reasons I can't determine moved to New York City in the 60s. So the themes of my rhymes move back and forth from country to city. As the rhymes accumulated on my hard drive, I occasionally submitted a collection to publishers (you've heard this before) and was always rejected. So at age seventy-six, it seemed time to self publish.

The rhymes are best sipped slowly a few at a time and not guzzled all at once. I hope they bring you a smile. Making people laugh is one step removed from saving their souls.

I've included at the end an old-fashioned hymn I wrote. As much as I love it, no church would give it a try, not even my local church choir. What fun to publish it here in spite of the naysayers.

Joann Sprangers Lee

Contents

Addiction 1
Adventure 1
After the Storm 1
Ah, to Nap 2
April Snow 2
Cactus 2
Alternate Pets 3
Camouflage 3
Baking Sweets 4
Blossoms 4
Bee-Fuddled 4
Balancing Act 5
Arrogance 5
Catch a Flight 6
Burger Alarm 6
Calendar Pages 6
Jimmied 7
Career Choice 7
Carma's Mansion 8
Cherry Snatcher 8
Carolee 9
Charged with Eternal Youth 9
Eau de Alcohol 9
Celebrity Causes 10
Caramel Apples 10
Chat 11
Chocolate Sense 11
Christmas Needles 12
Clothes Line 12
Natasha 12
Cloud of Suspicion 12

Christmas 1976 13
Daylight Saving 13
Collecting 14
Computer Forwards 14
Compared to Me 14
Coin Bank 15
Confetti 15
Corny 16
Parents that Drink 16
Daffodils Fenced 16
Correct Measure 17
Daffodil Beds 17
Curious Climb 18
Dandelion Bouquet 18
Dessert Control 19
Dandelion Pals 19
Fashion 19
Diet, Diet 20
Dangerous Block 20
Destiny 20
Costco in Wisconsin 21
Bus Germs 21
Deer Hunting 22
New Mom 22
Diet Logic 23
Food Choices 23
Dog in the Yard 24
Fakes 24
Elevator Sound Effects 25
Eyebrow Sketch 25
Eternity to Dust 26
Fashion Plate 26
Farmer's Wife 27

Dishwashing	27
Fast Worker	28
Darboy Tombstone	28
Fishing Conundrum	29
Gifts	29
Flowery Faces	30
Humor Divine	30
Frozen Lake	31
Evacuation Drill	31
Fundraiser	32
My Garden	33
Genius on Wing	33
Gift Exchange	34
Hare Brained	34
Gift from a Boss	35
Groups	36
Government Spending	36
Grudge	37
Hello, Good-bye	37
Hail Hail	38
Hang Up Your Clothes	38
Harmony	39
Heart Spare Part	39
Helen Won't Answer the Phone	39
Self Publish	40
Heavenly Rhymes	40
Hell's Bells	41
Glass Shard	41
It's Snow Cover	41
Hot Bus	42
I'd Love to Attend	42
Hindsight	42
Insults	43

It's Rhubarb	43
Late	44
Looking Back	44
La-Verne	45
Kris with the Smiling Face	46
Little Women	46
Look Alike	47
Maple Syruping	47
Maureen of Ireland	48
Mental Miles	49
My Funeral	49
My Weekend?	50
New York Storm	50
New Diet	51
No Gifts, Please	51
New Friend	52
On Hold	52
New York City Cow (Summer 2000)	53
Outspoken	53
New York Women	54
Opportunity	54
No Pets, Please	55
November Wedding	56
Onion	56
Org of the Orchard	57
Pen Points	57
Out of Biz	58
Party Pooper	58
Packing Light	59
Patience	59
Perfect Place to Work	60
Story Telling	60
Playwright's Lament	61

Potty Pose	62
Rainy Day	62
Priorities	63
Reincarnation	63
Reconfiguration	63
Rabbit Rides	64
Read a Book	65
Retiring	66
Rhyme Time	66
Ron S(hhh)	67
Senator	67
Sugared	68
James T of the North Woods	69
Rubber Boots	69
Seventy-Five	70
Shade	70
Shaky Seattle	71
Shoe Search	71
Silver Suit	72
Scotch Tape	72
Small Talk	73
Shopping	73
Smokes	74
Sonia	74
Snow Flake	75
Snow Predicted	75
So Long, Friend	76
Spidery Spin	76
Swim	76
Spring Ends	77
Spring Fever	77
Spring Heat Wave	77
Stephanie is Baking	78

Strategy	78
Stringy Bean	78
Stockings	79
Temperatures Rising	79
Sunrise	80
Sunset	80
Summer Linen	80
Weight Lost	80
Sweets Murder	81
Taxing	81
Taylor	82
Trees	82
Teapot from Pike's Market	83
Thinking Out Loud	83
When I Was Thin	83
Thrift Shop Apron	84
Unrequited	84
Voice	84
Trike Attack	85
Turtle Walk	85
Umbrella Shared	86
Violet Shy	86
Volunteer Anyone?	86
Walk in the City	87
Waterproofed	87
What an Old Lady Wears	88
When I Was Young	88
Which Way?	89
Wild Apples	89
Window West	89
Spain and France and Italy	90
Thank$	90
Words Anyone?	91

Woman in Red	92
Waiting Room	92
Apple Tree Pruner	93
Water a Melon	93
Ginny & Herb	94
Walk and Talk	94
When Death Comes to Call	95
Torch	96
Me, Myself or I?	97
Connie to Wed	98
Wish to Fish	98
Mighty Munching Man	99
Sara Bean	99
Small Town Girl	100
Andrea	101
And Now For The Song Section	102

Addiction

There is a distinction
Twixt drink and addiction
Though sometimes the boundaries are blurred.
I suggest you not think
It is harmless to drink
When already your words are all slurred.

Adventure

What happened to adventurous me
Who roamed the earth and sailed the sea?
I'd bring her back from who-knows-where
If I were not stuck in this chair.

After the Storm

The street is filled with skeletons
And shattered bits of skin.
A mighty battle they have lost
To see the shape they're in.
The sun now shines; the storm is past.
They once sailed overhead—
Now lie in tatters on the street,
Umbrellas torn and dead.

Ah, to Nap

If ever I should fall asleep and it is still mid-day
An anti-nap phenomenon comes quickly into play.
A beacon through the stratosphere tells friends and family
That it is time to dial the phone and have a chat with me.
So when you feel the urge to dial for a quick "hello"
First sit down and read the paper for an hour or so.

April Snow

An April snowstorm has arrived.
A few tough daffodils survived.
Though yesterday was sunny spring
We'd given clocks their forward swing.
The clocks and weather were bewitched,
Because that night the seasons switched
With winter storming its way in
And caring not how spring it's been.

Cactus

My cactus plant is sweet and shy.
It grabs my skirt as I walk by.

Alternate Pets

Perfect pets are always cute and sometimes useful too.
A pet cow gives its owner more than just a friendly moo.
Fresh milk and cream that you can whip, plus make exotic cheese.
And what a fertilizer to encourage backyard trees!
But pet cows make a few demands; you milk them twice a day,
Which means you get no time away, no not a single day.
A cow has need of ample space which may be rather hard,
Particularly if you do not have a spacious yard.
Perhaps a chicken is preferred as quite a useful pet.
It lays its eggs most every day and seldom needs a vet.
It won't demand affection when you are not in the mood.
Its eggs are filled with protein and make most nutritious food.
A chicken is a problem when you're in the house with it.
It cannot be housebroken, so there's always chicken shit.
A soft and cuddly rabbit would be quite a lovely pet.
They do not jump and lick on you and get your face all wet.
They're cute and very cuddly and will not pester you.
And when you have grown sick of them, they make a tasty stew.

Camouflage

Ah yes, I'm old but what the heck.
A good scarf hides a wrinkled neck.

Baking Sweets

They wake on Sunday morning to the smell of baking sweets,
Of cookies, breads, and muffins, cakes and lots of yummy treats.
How much they'd like to leap from bed, rush out and eat it all.
Unfortunately I'm the baker; they live down the hall.

Blossoms

The town was dressed in blossoms
For as far as eye could see.
All tethered to the earth in clouds of pink and ivory.
I hoped the town would hold them tight
And blossomed days would stay.
But when I stepped outside today,
They "poof" had blown away.

Bee-Fuddled

A bunch of bees went buzzing by.
They zigged and zagged to left and right.
They could not find their favorite blooms.
I put them in a vase last night.

Balancing Act

Of all of nature's mysteries this is the greatest one,
And when I see it daily always wonder how it's done.
A man so wide and very tall,
How does he balance and not fall?
He walks all day on little feet
But seldom falls flat on the street.
No matter what his height and girth
His feet remain affixed to earth.
I watch you walking down the street
On what are much too teeny feet.
I watch in wonder knowing that
Reality should knock you flat.

Arrogance

She's arrogant, they say of me, her self-opinion high.
Most of my siblings are the same. I often wonder why.
I look around at cousins from my father's family.
They're all more self-assured and louder than they need to be.
Is there some strain of boastfulness found in our DNA?
Not that we'd change it if we could. It's fun to be this way!

Catch a Flight

The airline website clearly said
Arrive at least three hours ahead.
"Whoa!" I thought, but said, "Okay."
I follow orders. I obey.
Quickly I sped through the line.
One hour would have been just fine.
The airline told a big fat lie
So now I sit and wait to fly.

Burger Alarm

A burger and some fries—
Oh what a nice surprise.
You're filled with juicy fat
And salt, a ton of that!
My pleasure would increase
If all those warnings cease.
Deliciousness full tilt
With Burgers but no guilt.

Calendar Pages

The calendar pages are flipping so fast;
Last year had just started and now it is past.

Jimmied

Jimmy, Jimmy what's he done—
Rhymed an email just for fun.
Rog and Joann work all day.
To rhyme each single thing they say.
No word from those with no time
To turn their emails into rhyme.

Career Choice

When I arrived at Amex a big choice was given me:
Become a low Admin Assist or right up to VP.
I walked the Amex halls to see which group best suited me.
Associates showed jolly grins and chatted happily.
If someone looked too serious, I knew, yup, some VP.
But VPs have the power and the big fat salary.
I am a little power hungry and a bit greedy.
But would I rather talk to Phyllis, Kathy or May Lee,
To Erika or Lorie? Or some stressed-out VP.
As I was just about to choose, a voice mail came to me.
They did not want a VP here who writes dumb poetry.
Well, they can keep that VP spot. It's quite all right with me.
I'd rather be a low admin for all eternity.

Carma's Mansion

Carma bought a mansion with some windows—sixty-eight.
Carma has not moved in yet, but she can hardly wait.
Carma loves to polish glass—it has some French doors, too.
Carma can't come to the phone, she has some work to do.

Carma bought a Yonkers mansion with some bedrooms—six.
Carma bought a mansion that has lots of stuff to fix.
Carma bought a mansion that has lots of rooms to heat.
Carma cannot pay for that and buy some food to eat.

Carma bought a Yonkers mansion with some bathrooms—five.
Carma will not live in some low-class four-bathroom dive.
Carma has some dusting rags, a vacuum, Windex, too.
Carma can't come out to play, she has some work to do.

Cherry Snatcher

Bouquet of snow white blossoms it hands you in the spring,
Then gifts of bright red cherries, those tart and tasty things!
A miracle of nature with fruit and flowers, too,
Then thieving robin red-breast steals every one from you.

Carolee

Who is the sweetest person in my lifelong memory?
There is one name that comes to mind and that is Carolee.
She always makes you smile when she pops into your view,
And looks just like an angel, though she's had misfortune too.
Through trial and tribulation, she turns to God and prayer,
And shows by her example how we all should love and care.
I wonder if there's any chance in some lifetime I'll be
As kind and sweet and beautiful as our own Carolee.
But not to be too greedy, if all this cannot be,
I'll take just her good looks and leave the rest to Carolee.

Charged with Eternal Youth

Photo on my charge card? Young and pretty, as you see.
A picture snapped by Citibank way back in '83.
Expiration of the card can change from year-to-year,
But not my face unless, that is, I look into the mirror.

Eau de Alcohol

You think we don't know that you drink
But you exude the dreadful stink
Of yesterday's dead alcohol
That overwhelms us in the hall.

Celebrity Causes

Celebrities, you love to preach
And give us all your rain forest speech.
You want us to save dwindling trees
And save that ozone layer, please.
You chide us with your master plan
To save the earth from common man.
I noticed your immense estate
Protected with an iron gate.
Your mansion's many rooms at night
Give off a thousand beams of light.
What is the cost to heat and cool
That huge estate with swimming pool?
Good conservation has to start
With sacrifices on your part.
While in the lap of luxury
Don't preach environment to me,
Unless our wealth should equalize
And I can also sermonize.

Caramel Apples

Round red apples, crunchy, white
Fill the orchard, awesome sight.
Tasty eaten off the tree.
Even better caramel-y.

Chat

Doctor said leukemia.
My son was only two.
Try so early to leave me?
I just gave birth to you.

What can be the reason why
You want to leave so fast?
Hang around and chat a while.
Let's make this visit last.

So he did and so we talked
Until at twenty-five.
He made a move to out-of-state
But this time stayed alive.

Chocolate Sense

I love the smell of chocolate.
I love its creamy taste.
I only hope, dear chocolate,
You do not go to waist.

Christmas Needles

It was a perfect Christmas tree
Adorned and dearly loved by me.
I do not love it any more.
It threw its needles on my floor.

Clothes Line

Once clothes were pinned on lines outside
And carried in when fluffed and dried.
Now driers get the exercise
And dry clothes of increasing size.

Natasha

I went to find Natasha when I saw some plates of food,
Because I know Natasha's always in a munching mood.
I went to find Natasha, but Natasha was not there.
She was not at her desk today, so I ate Tasha's share.

Cloud of Suspicion

A single fluffy cloud drifts slowly through the clear blue sky.
What keeps that puff of moisture floating when the air is dry?
I stand and stare suspiciously and watch it move so slow.
Is this a clever camouflage for sneaky UFO?

Christmas 1976

It was a sad Christmas as Christmases go
Though nothing to do with tradition or snow.
For between his birthday and holiday fun,
Leukemia dropped off its gift to my son.
He was just a baby, he was only two.
With such devastation, what's mother to do?
I cooked Christmas dinner. We ate it (instead
Of at home) on Greg's hospital bed.
On the other small bed in the room a sweet sight,
Ignoring the darkness with colorful light.
A gingerbread house by a sister of mine,
Nadine with her talent for clever design.
Bright windows of melted Life Savers all lit.
I'll never forget the enchantment of it.
It proves that no matter how grim life can be,
You always can drop in a sweet memory.

Daylight Saving

I hate the modern custom when we turn the clocks ahead
To push me out an hour early from my comfy bed.

Collecting

Overburdened with his stuff, Seventeenth Street homeless man,
His three rolling canvas carts filled with junk, his moving van.
All three carts were overflowing with bags hanging on the side.
Human instinct to collect too much junk on life's short ride.
Scornfully I looked at him. How much freer he would be
Unencumbered by the junk. Oh, oh, that's also true of me.

Computer Forwards

No matter how clever you think they may be,
I do not like forwards. Don't send them to me.
A strange hidden virus may melt my PC.
If you think they're funny, please laugh without me.

Compared to Me

I neither like comparisons nor like to make a fuss.
There's not a lot of difference between the two of us.
I'm taller, smarter, better looking than the likes of you.
You're shorter, dumber, homelier. And I am humble, too.

Coin Bank

Don't save your pennies in a jar,
Or folks will know you've not gone far
Financially toward success
And may be in some cash distress.
Financial planning? Don't admit
You have a big glass jug for it.
Successful men respect their cash
And find the wisest place to stash
Each penny carefully away
Where it builds interest every day.
To someday join those in the pink,
You'll have to change the way you think.
That's free advice; please, not a hug.
Just throw some quarters in my jug.

Confetti

Alleluia! Here's confetti
Sprinkled on your restaurant floor.
Chopped up from those dratted menus
Under my apartment door.

Corny

Corn tassels waving to me.
Open the cobs and peer in.
Kernels lined up in a row
Give me a big corny grin.

Parents that Drink

Parents that drink
Are inclined to think
That drinking's a barrel of fun.
The same is not true
Of me and of you
If we are their daughter or son.

Daffodils Fenced

Imprisoned little daffodils are peering through the bars,
Shining from a distance like some sunny yellow stars,
Nod and sway and plan escape from their cold prison beds,
Little knowing in a week they all will lose their heads.

Correct Measure

A row of cups for measuring hangs neatly on my wall
But with the slightest bump unhook and cling clang as they fall.
Their little stainless bottoms have had lots of banging bumps
And all have indentations in their shiny little rumps.
Inspecting all the many dimples I can plainly see
They won't precisely measure with reliability.
It's hard discerning what is lost in cups from this abuse.
They cannot be relied upon for scientific use.
Must I recalculate the wet and dry ingredients
To take into account the size of those substantial dents?
To discard all my loyal cups would be a dreadful shame.
I wrinkled up the recipes. Now everything's the same.

Daffodil Beds

Too many of you daffodils with puffy yellow heads.
You hog too much attention as you pack the flower beds.
You cannot wait for tulips that might add diversity,
But push the bounds of spring each year and bloom impatiently.
Every morning in the spring I view your flower bed
With cheery heart to know that soon you'll all be dried and dead.

Curious Climb

What will I see over top of the hill?
Will its other side be a new scenic thrill?
Perhaps there's a glorious, exquisite view
Of new wildernesses seen just by a few?
I plow through the trees and the brush to get there.
I go up a hundred more feet in the air.
I plunge ever onward and ever ahead
Through briars and brambles and thorns that I dread.
I finally am on this steep hill's very top.
My skin torn and bloody; feet covered with slop.
Success should now fill my whole soul with great pride,
But there's only brush on the hill's other side.

Dandelion Bouquet

When I was young the hill beyond
The school yard and the old fish pond
In spring, a painted yellow hill
Of dandelions, so I would fill
My fist full with a tight nosegay
And hope to cheer up mother's day.
I did not know they were not prized
But she would always act surprised,
She'd take my proudly held display
And thank me for the weed bouquet.

Dessert Control

It's self control if I don't take
A giant piece of that cheesecake.
It's self-indulgent if I do
Perhaps a trifle fattening, too.

Dandelion Pals

Humble little dandelion,
You are a favorite friend of mine.
I love to see your yellow heads
Pop unannounced in flower beds.
You toss yourselves across the lawn
With sunny faces bright as dawn.
You effortlessly sprout at will
Without the prod of gardener's skill.
Although you're yanked out and maligned,
I'm still a fan of dandelion.
You show me how I too can be
Determined, tough, yet flowery

Fashion

I never notice what you wear
Because I'm fashion unaware.
"Dress for Dummies" would indeed
Be just the guidance that I need.

Diet, Diet

Once again I'll try to diet
Well, at least I'll try to try it.
All my waistbands are too tight,
So the time is always right.
Yummy food I will ignore.
Well, of course, I've tried before.
Will I lose a pound or so?
If I'm betting, I'll take "no".

Dangerous Block

It is with trepidation that I saunter down that street,
With heightened apprehension at the challenge I will meet.
It will be difficult protecting my small wad of cash
On a block with three thrift shops all filled with tempting trash.

Destiny

You cannot fight your destiny
And be what you're not meant to be,
No matter how aggressively
You storm the heavens with your plea.
Stop wailing so dramatically!
You're drowning out the cries from me.

Costco in Wisconsin

(This was written before Costco finally opened in WI.)
Though Costco is the place to go,
In my home state, it is not so.
Not one found in our great state.
Guess the cheese-heads do not rate.
Every month I scan the list.
Is there something I have missed?
Did one open in Green Bay?
Sorry, no, I'm sad to say.
Hayward, Oshkosh, Peewaukee?
Wauwatosa, Milwaukee?
In West Allis, Appleton?
Weyauwega? None, none, none.
No Wisconsin on the list.
They don't know that we exist.
Til things change I guess I am
Forced to stick with Sam I am.

Bus Germs

The bus filled with bacteria, the travelers take a ride
With humid, stale and fetid air all bundled up inside.
Sore throats and colds and flu and coughs mixed in the putrid air.
It all sounds so inviting. Shall we take a bus somewhere?

Deer Hunting

It is an old tradition, going hunting in the fall.
A few of my six brothers, as loud as they are tall,
Will head up for deer country leaving wives and kids behind.
And though they miss Thanksgiving, no one seems much to mind.
They settle in a cottage on a little northern lake.
A few of them like cooking, a couple of them bake.
Real purpose of the journey should be to hunt the deer.
There is a little question though how often they appear
Out in the cold and bitter northern woods to hunt or stalk,
Or wait in those cold bushes or take long hunting walks.
They eat and drink and cook and laugh and play a little cards
And sometimes glance through windows as a big buck strolls the yard.
Should one of them quite accidently shoot a deer,
The wives complain tough venison hogs freezer space that year.
Great traditions that they love repeated every year.
When these great hunters hit the woods the deer have naught to fear.

New Mom

It's fun to have a baby; yes, it's fun, fun, fun,
Except fatigue and work are never done, done, done.
So try to sleep a lot while he/she is not here.
For when he/she arrives I sadly fear, fear, fear
Your nights of restful sleep will all be done, done, done,
And you'll be much too weary for that fun, fun, fun.

Diet Logic

By what bizarre and crazy logic do I stuff my face—
Five seconds joy for taste buds but ten years of plump disgrace.
I eat and seconds later stand in horror at the mirror
And wish that my pot belly would by magic disappear.
I scratch my head in wonder at the ever-growing size
Of clothes that fill my closet that I purchased to disguise
That I've been eating way too much of all things good and bad.
By analyzing what went wrong, I now am very glad
That with this logic I am sure my pounds will melt away.
But first I'll finish off the donuts that I bought today.

Food Choices

There's yogurt in its carton,
And wheat germ in its jar.
The lettuce in its plastic bag
Won't get me very far.
Deciding is so difficult—
Which healthy thing to eat.
So while I do some pondering,
I'll munch on something sweet.

Joann Sprangers Lee

Dog in the Yard

This tale would be hard to conceive.
It is one you may not believe.
I went to Wisconsin last week
To rest and recoup so to speak.
Sister Marian works very hard
To maintain her dog and her yard.
The dog does not have lots of class
So drops his turds onto the grass,
So when the long grass must be cut
She must clean up after that mutt.
Across the large lawn she zigzags –
Dropping turds in plastic bags.
The other choice? Let them amass
And chop them up with the green grass.

Fakes

Artificial flowers I see you left for me.
You're a fake and they're a fake, so how appropriately.
You have much in common, so appealing—look so real.
As always I am taken in with bits of eye appeal.

Elevator Sound Effects

An attractive blonde was on my elevator ride.
Moving up some forty floors we traveled side-by-side.
From the cafeteria from which her trip began
She clutched a bowl of cereal in her dainty hand.
From the bowl with delicate fingers she would take
In her mouth and munch each little sugar frosted flake.
Hear the noisy sound effects one hungry blonde can make
Early in the morning with a sugar frosted flake.

Eyebrow Sketch

God was the master of detail when He designed the face
And sketched on each of us two eyebrows in the proper place,
An excellent example of the most unusual care
That He took in creating us to place two commas there.
For were they somehow both erased to leave our foreheads bare,
Our photos would all sorely miss those little clumps of hair.
Divine attention to detail impresses me, and yet
God somehow did not manage to make mine a matching set.

Eternity to Dust

If my soul is eternal (and I do believe that's true),
Why am I always rushing with a million things to do?
If I am so eternal with forever down the road,
Should I not take the extra time to ease this heavy load?
Should I take time to contemplate and stare off into space
And take a long break from the frenzy of this human race?
I wonder if it matters in eternity's broad view
If I should clean my house today or sit and chat with you?
And do I need those luxuries that chain me to the plow?
Just where will all my worries be a hundred years from now?
If I were a philosopher I'd scan eternal skies
And press my soul for answers to eternal how's and why's.
I'd like to take the broader view, but for today I must
Stop all this idle chit-chat because I have to dust.

Fashion Plate

Fashions come and fashions go.
What's in style? I do not know.
I've never had a fashion eye.
I never know what I should buy.
I sometimes stumble into style,
Accidentally, for a while.
But when I'm out and people stare.
I do not know and do not care.

Farmer's Wife

Millie is a farmer's wife, who worked hard on the farm.
Millie's hands are gnarled hands, her arms strong farmer arms.
Her face is creased and wrinkled and her hair sun-dried and gray.
Mike and Millie dressed and worked like farmhands every day.
But then good fortune came to call and subdivide the farm
With cul-de-sacs, split levels, and a switch to urban charm.
Their bank account is heavy and the farm has turned to gold,
But it's too late for them to change, they're tired and they're old.
They still look like old farmhands, but they've changed one minor thing.
Milly's gnarled hand now sports a carat diamond ring.

Dishwashing

The trauma of the dirty dish still haunts me every day.
A nightmare of my childhood—dishes, dishes in my way.
I was the oldest child of twelve. My mother loved to cook
A ton of breads and cakes and pies, which made our kitchen look
Much like the busy galley of a giant battle ship
That could feed several thousand on an ocean-going trip.
So every dish and every spoon and every pot and pan
Were used in everything she made and that left poor Joann
With tortured hours year-by-year each morning, noon, and night
To wash the ninety trillion dishes everywhere in sight.
I tell this sordid tale in hope you'll grant my fondest wish,
That on my visit you won't let me wash a single dish.

Fast Worker

The fastest and the slowest are often paid the same
All based upon their title, not how they play the game.
You can produce a ton or more while neighbors down the hall
Will sit and twiddle thumbs, producing little work at all.
There's not a tool to measure that I do more than my share,
Producing more than twice as much as that old poke down there.
Since you oppose the increase that would double my small pay,
I know you won't complain if I work only half a day.

Darboy Tombstone

My name is on a tombstone and it is not even mine.
It's strange to see your name so somber when you're feeling fine.
And so much better to be carved upon this other tomb
As offspring of the pair that long ago were bride and groom.
All fourteen names upon that stone, my mother and my dad,
A dozen sons and daughters in the family they had.
There's something permanent and solid being carved in stone
That binds us all perpetually, like rock, not flesh and bone.
I wonder if it might long stand just like the pyramids
Ten-thousand years of testament for mom, dad and us kids.

Fishing Conundrum

It's so much fun to cast for fish—
Float on the water with the wish
That soon your very well-placed cast
Will hook a big prize-winning bass,
Or even some much smaller fish
To fill this evening's dinner dish.
It's great suspense, the gambler's wait,
The hope that fish will take your bait.
You use live bait or plastic one—
In either case, tremendous fun.
It's floating on a summer lake
With all the time you want to take.
It's watching clouds go breezing by
In water mirroring the sky.
I have one final little wish,
That it was fun to clean the fish.

Gifts

That gift you gave me is superb.
I would expand some on this blurb
But I must pack your gift away.
The Goodwill truck is on its way.

Flowery Faces

When spring appears I get depressed and sick of this rat race
And long to leave the city for some green and open space.
And every year the same old thing, I grumble and I groan.
I want a little piece of land and garden of my own.
I long for country living and some backyard apple trees,
Some lettuce and tomatoes and a little patch of peas,
A field of flowers to provide a multi-colored view.
Then one year I heard whispered, "There is special news for you."
A special message for me that was sent from up above,
"The best of my creation is right here for you to love.
My people are the loveliest of all the flowers made,
And New York is packed full of them in every size and shade."
I tried to take the good advice that God had given me
And view the signs of spring in March a little differently.
His people are quite cute, I guess, but if the truth be known,
I'd trade them all for country life and garden of my own.

Humor Divine

At Burger King for lunch one day, this question crossed my mind,
Though steeped in deep philosophy, the answer hard to find.
Has God a sense of humor? Hmm, that question is profound!
"How could I not?" He quickly answered, "Take a look around."

Frozen Lake

I watched out the cottage window for days
And peered at the frozen lake
And waited for spring and the ice to melt
And wondered how long it would take.
It's taking forever, it's taking forever
Became my persistent lament.
As I looked away a split second one day,
It was gone. Do you know where it went?
It was much too thick to have melted that fast,
Not easy dissolving that mass.
I strongly suspect like a giant ice cube
It sunk down a bit in the glass.

Evacuation Drill

Evacuation? Wow, what fun.
Forty stories one-by-one.
What a sporting thing to do!
Gee, I'd like to walk with you!
But alas, don't look for me.
I must leave early, say at three.

Fundraiser

We're throwing a lunch.
We hope for a bunch
Of people with money—like you.
Though logic dictates
That piling your plates
Might not be the wise thing to do.
The money we spend
Should really all end
In charities' coffers. That's giving!
Not be spent on food
Putting you in the mood
By indulging your gluttonous living.
Orgs needing your care
Will have some reps there
Explaining the meeting's real goal.
So come if you will
Knowing that you can fill
Not only your stomach—but soul.

My Garden

Each morning I admire my lovely flowered yard
And gaze amazed at all of it and often find it hard
Believing how well it is done,
From giant fountain in the sun
To all the plants artistically
Arranged so complementarily.
Surely I've a gardener who deserves his hefty pay
To primp and mow and sweat beneath the hot sun every day.
But I pretend I own it and somehow did it all,
As every morning I walk through the park at City Hall.

Genius on Wing

Genius is hated and genius is scorned,
Especially when genius is not well-adorned
With trappings of genius we've come to expect,
Like white beards and glasses and such smart effects.
I've seen some great geniuses fly overhead,
That you too may see if you toss down some bread.
The pigeons, invisible seconds before,
Now fly in with radar, some fifty or more.
And only a genius could play their smart game
Of swift aeronautics and on-target aim.
Last week I was raising my hand from my lap.
They made it a target and bombed pigeon crap.

Joann Sprangers Lee

Gift Exchange

Closets filled? You've no more space?
For all your years you've packed your place
With kitschy geegaws, trinkets, trash.
All take up space and waste your cash.
The endless, useless, cheerful junk
That lies unused in drawer or trunk,
Or gathers dust a while until
It's packed and shipped off to Goodwill.
Though all around can plainly see
You need a new philosophy
Of gift exchanges that won't lead
To crap you do not use or need.
Those gifts you eat or drink today
Surpass those that we stash away.
The gift that's best and loved a lot
Must be consumed or it will rot.

Hare Brained

My brain is a turtle surrounded by hares.
My brain works a fraction as fast as all theirs.
If I disagree with the hares when they speak,
My answer is brilliant but takes me a week.

Gift from a Boss

I had a boss who treated me
Like I was two or maybe three,
When I was half a century.
One Christmas he passed on to me
A gift from some book company
Displaying country scenery,
A most unusual fabric bag
With hunting scene, horse, fence and stag.
I loved that bag, which handily
Carried lunch and books for me.
The boss and job are now long past,
Forgotten, too, were I not asked
So constantly about the bag,
"How interesting with fence and stag."
"Where did you get it?" they'd ask me.
From a boss who treated me
Like I was two or maybe three
When I was half a century.

Groups

I hate group activities.
I like one or two—
An intimate chit chat
Between me and you.
The larger the group is
The more I will balk.
Cause that means that I'll have
Much less chance to talk.

Government Spending

Be careful how you spend my money, Mr. Government.
Before I even earn the dough, you have the tax all spent.
The debt is in the trillions and you still are spending more
And often take a junket to exotic distant shore.
Was thriftiness left out when you were taught at mother's knee?
Now we must pay for her neglect with debt economy.
While you are pouring money into a strange dictator's purse,
Conditions for the citizens continue to get worse.
It seems a little common sense should now be put to use,
Unless I get elected and can join in the abuse.

Grudge

Grudge, oh grudge, hold on to them though they will take a toll.
They'll beat up your relationships and wound your heart and soul.
You hold the pain and hurt inside and guard it carefully,
Then use a perceived insult to cut friends or family.
You've harbored deep dark hurts that festered, growing over time
Then strike out anywhere to punish someone for the crime.
I've noticed that old grudges stick to people in great pain,
Who have been wounded psychically, then buckle with the strain.
They are so wounded deep inside by yet some other hand,
That just the slightest added tap is more than they can stand.
They're overwhelmed and bury all the hurt deep in their soul,
Where it ferments locked deep away to take its vengeful toll.
The chances are the pain will build and never go away
And tightly grip the wounded soul until its dying day.
So when the body's laid to rest and all of life seems past,
Soul's pain rides to the other side because it's built to last.

Hello, Good-bye

I called you just to say hello
But you refused to let me go.
Should hell freeze over, that is when
I'll make a friendly call again.

Hail Hail

Hail season is plotting and casting its eye
On apple trees from its cold perch in the sky.
It's hoping to ding every apple it can
To leave Orchard Org a most frustrated man.
There is a defense from this terrible ding.
We must turn to God with some praying each spring.
But as once before when the weather was grim
And I recommended a few prayers from him,
He'll likely suggest in my brother's old way,
"I have an idea. I'll watch while you pray."

Hang Up Your Clothes

Monday, Tuesday, Wednesday, Thursday, Friday on the chair,
Layered day-by-day my wardrobe, what I chose to wear.
Can't build up the energy to hang my clothes at night.
Saturday a nightmare and the bedroom is a sight.
Nasty habit of my youth returned to haunt my soul.
Dead and gone is any chance for neatness as my goal.
As I sit and ponder the solution that I seek,
Think I'll just relax and hang them every other week.

Harmony

Were life and I in harmony,
I would look like a willow tree.
I'd gracefully adorn the earth
And have a lithesome, dainty girth.
I'm not that slender, swaying tree
That I intended me to be.
I ate a bit too much, you see,
And made a small balloon of me.

Heart Spare Part

On occasion worn-out hearts
Require patching with spare parts.
My valve wore out and was a mess—
Replacement needed I confess.
Alas in this old heart of mine
A brand new valve that is bovine,

Helen Won't Answer the Phone

Helen is all frazzled because Helen cannot sleep.
Helen can't pick up the phone. The stairs are much too steep.
Helen cannot speak right now. Helen's flat in bed.
Helen doesn't want the news unless somebody's dead.

Joann Sprangers Lee

Self Publish

I'll self-publish all my rhymes
I told myself a hundred times.
It surely will be lots of fun.
Okay, folks, here's how it's done?
The rules to publish if you please
The same with most pub companies.
To read the fine-print you must squint
Then pay them up-front first to print.
You pay them for each book you buy
And pay for shipping, my-oh-my.
They hold for three months what you make.
Then lot more time than it should take —
Yes, sixty days to write your check.
Zero interest. What the heck.
I will find this really funny
If they don't make all the money.

Heavenly Rhymes

Does heaven have a language
And if so does it rhyme?
I otherwise do not know what
I'll do there with my time.

Hell's Bells

It happens even in the train
(My friends have all heard me complain)
That any time I fall asleep
And hope no one will make a peep,
I barely nod off when hell's bells
Peal out from seatmates' dratted cells.

Glass Shard

A shard of glass is in my foot,
I feel it when I stand.
Podiatrists have searched for it.
Where did that rascal land?
It's hiding out and pokes at me
When I go strolling round.
It is more clever than us all
And never may be found.

It's Snow Cover

God took all day to cover up the ugly parts of town.
I watched in wonder and delight as banks of snow poured down.
His mission was accomplished, but it lasted just one day,
For when He rolled the sun back out, His cover dripped away.

Hot Bus

So often we are tortured by the driver of the bus
Who alternately tries to freeze, then cook the life from us.
When temp outside is one-oh-one, the bus is 55.
But worse yet is the winter bus where you are steamed alive.
All bundled in December duds, you're dressed for winter streets,
But in the bus your perspiration dribbles on the seats.
The driver with his rolled up sleeves is comfy as he greets
Another group of victims from the freezing city streets.
I'd someday like to see that driver sweat like all of us
If there's a place in the hereafter hotter than a bus.

I'd Love to Attend

I've always been much of a loner—
In large crowds hide in the dark corner.
But I will attend this event,
Pretending I'm glad that I went.
My face will look glad to be there,
But my mind will be off who knows where.

Hindsight

If I were thirty and could see
A photo of the right-now me.
I would have taken much more pain
Avoiding all that blubber gain.

Insults

I notice they make fun of me
Because I'm old and gray
And don't remember what I wrote
And rhymed just yesterday.
The insults don't seem quite as mean
As insults are sometime,
Because they are remembering
To make the insults rhyme.

It's Rhubarb

There's lots of talk of rhubarb in the family mail these days.
They're cooking up those sour stalks in quite creative ways.
In cakes it's laced with sour cream, in pies with fatty crust.
For others it's the tartly torte with ice cream as a must.
But unlike you I do not have a backyard rhubarb plant.
My window sill container space is growing somewhat scant.
It's also disconcerting to mix up a batch of dough
Whose sugar content as percent is ninety-five or so.

Late

She always comes late,
A habit I hate.
For lunch or for show
She moves much too slow.
My foot taps the floor
Eyes glued to the door,
I'd throw a small fit
If I never did it.

Looking Back

It's quite a strange perspective as I view life from this end
And recognize some things I did were not the way to spend
A very finite chunk of time. I watched too much TV.
I can't recall a single show that meant that much to me.
I now know that the silly things have brought the greatest joys,
Like filling Gregory's bedroom with too many chirpy toys.
When I rewind and view my days in snippets here and there,
What tops the list are all the laughs that I've been blessed to share.
I hope for laughs in heaven with the funny folks I've known.
If you won't be in heaven, leave me the hell alone.

La-Verne

(A co-worker with outfits in head-to-toe color)
Who's that lady dressed in red
From her soles up to her head?
With a hyphen in her name?
La-dash-Verne of office fame.
Project deadline growing near?
La-dash-Verne will volunteer.
Have a meeting—you can't speak?
Meetings make your knees go weak?
Here's exactly what to do.
Let La-dash-Verne speak for you.
Audiences stop and stare
As her hands wave in the air.
She will stare straight at your boss
And get your ideas across.
You have some big project due?
Who can find the facts for you?
Super-charged and dressed in blue,
La-dash-Verne is there for you.
Need a luncheon organized,
Just for two or super-sized?
She's the dining-menu whiz,
Knows where each swell restaurant is.
Tired of being mild and meek?
Want her pizzazz when you speak?
Add a hyphen to your name.
Then we all will be the same.
Le-dash-ona, Jo-dash-ann
Get the picture, get the plan?
One more thing you'll have to do.
Dress entirely in blue.

Joann Sprangers Lee

Kris with the Smiling Face

Steve married a girl with a bright smiling face
That often can light up the most dreary place.
I've seen many faces in my many years,
Both faces of smiles and faces of tears.
But rarely I've seen a face smiling like this.
Though all faces smile, it is seldom like Kris.
I sit and ponder what the reason might be
That one smile can beam out so radiantly.
I think I have figured out one reason why.
Through many past lifetimes with clouds in the sky
She tried hard to brighten each sad person's day
And threw some smile sunshine when things seemed too gray.
She smiled as she met each new person and place.
That habit of smiling now shows on her face.

Little Women

I work with little women at American Express.
They're all well-educated and wear office casual dress.
They pack in elevators and then scurry on their way
To all the many meetings they have scheduled every day.
I feel a little out-of-place; the reason is three-fold.
They're mostly short-thin-young, while I am mostly tall-fat-old.

Look Alike

I know someone who looks like you
But I cannot remember who.
Each time I see you in the hall
(Although we've never met at all)
I see great similarity
And wonder what the names could be.
Two faces looking much the same
But neither of you has a name.

Maple Syruping

Warm days, cold nights. It's time to tap
The maples. Drip, drip, drip of sap.
The rhythmic drum of northern springs,
Sweet memories that syruping brings
Of steaming cookers, sugared air,
The amber syrup extraordinaire.
I left behind the maple trees
And maple-scented April breeze.
Instead of trees with sweet largess,
There's traffic, sirens, EMS.
No sweet drip, drip from maple tap.
I had a choice and chose this crap.

Joann Sprangers Lee

Maureen of Ireland

You left your native country for this far and distant land
And then became an actress, doing roles both small and grand.
You're in the city with us all, and you're far, far from home—
Far, far from all the Irish hills and rocky shore and loam.
And your daughter Oona with the blue eyes and black hair
Has moved herself to Ireland and loves it over there.
Although you love the opera and sing most every day
And cast your eyes to heaven 'cause you really love to pray,
All of your friends are drooping, as they get old, plump and gray.
They'll all be dropping by the wayside almost any day.
You're stuck now in this city, where you look east to the sea
And squint and look to Ireland where soon you want to be.
Maureen, now you're plotting and you're thinking here of late
How to get back to Ireland, reverse the course of fate.
Yes, someday soon you will head back to Ireland's green shore.
Just like a boomerang you're aiming eastward out of the door.
I have a little message though before you say good-bye.
I know a lot of people who will miss your apple pie.

Mental Miles

Bad news came and inked a stain
As black as grief across my brain.
I set about determinedly
To soothe my short term memory
With mental miles of sweeter things
Than those that bitter news oft brings.
I made some calls with laugh and talk
And took a lengthy, scene-filled walk.
I browsed in cluttered knick-knack shops
And made a few fun munching stops.
I clicked a million mental shots
That blotted out those inky spots
That soon were just the dust that lined
The bottom of my smiling mind.

My Funeral

I've been to many funerals where mourners pack each pew.
I sadly fear that when I die the mourners will be few.
There's more to death than dying that has me feeling low,
All the people that I know will fill perhaps one row.
Then add the priest and organist and that's who will be there.
Hey wait. I will be dead. The church is empty? I won't care!

Joann Sprangers Lee

My Weekend?

How was my weekend? It was fine,
Although I'm weary of that line.
I don't see why you really care
About the what or when or where.
How was my weekend? My reply
Is probably a big fat lie.
If you insist on being nice
"Hello" is quick and will suffice.
One other subject that I hate:
And my vacation? It was great.

New York Storm

I dressed today for ten-below
With knee-high boots for all the snow.
But out the door to my surprise
I sweat beneath the sunny skies.
The snow escaped in dark-of-night—
And spring came hand-in-hand with light.

New Diet

I devised a new menu and gleefully tried it,
A unique, creative and guaranteed diet,
With bits of granola throughout the day
Whenever my stomach was gnawing away.
It seemed fairly painless and not a big deal.
I launched into weight loss with simpleton's zeal.
But down in the footnotes of my diet plan
I listed exceptions (as you'll understand)
For special events when to diet would be
Unfriendly or food was too tempting for me.
A friend's invitation for pasta and such,
A cheesecake or chocolate, I won't eat too much.
But too late I found out, unfortunately,
Those special occasions are fattening me.

No Gifts, Please

Don't give me gifts, I have no room.
They'll be here 'til I'm in the tomb.
I can't dispose or give away.
They'll be here to my dying day.
Instead of littering my shelf,
Try keeping that junk for yourself.

New Friend

Will you be my brand new friend?
I need a new one—need to spend
A few hours laughing at new lines.
I'm bored with those old friends of mine.
I've heard the stories, know the score.
I've heard ten thousand times before.
A friend can be a treasured joy,
But they wear out like corduroy.
So you and I will be true blue
And best friends 'til I'm sick of you.

On Hold

Lined up like dragonflies, head toe, head toe,
Waiting to take off, all waiting to go.
But at LaGuardia patiently stand,
Stuck on the runway, on hold, stuck on land.
Just like my life, I was watching the sky
And waiting for someone to say, "Okay, fly."

With a Twist of Rhyme

New York City Cow (Summer 2000)

(In 2000 life-sized cow statues were placed around town)
Twelve-fifty-one Sixth Avenue—each noon upon the wall
Around a large reflecting pool the lunchers sit and sprawl
Their legs while lunch is carefully balanced on their knees,
And at their feet a full-sized cow contented as you please.
It's all in white with yellow daisies growing up its side,
Just like a pet that any owner would display with pride.
Yes, so alike another pet reclining from its play
I half expect to see it trail its owner home one day.
This cow is more appealing than the cows that I recall
That occupied Wisconsin fields and farms when I was small,
That pooped and swished their dirty tails to keep the flies away,
And never would just lie around to watch us kids at play.
I much prefer the beauty of this brand new city cow,
If only it could find a way to give us milk somehow.

Outspoken

They say I'm self-righteous, they say I'm too proud.
They say I'm outspoken, they say I'm too loud.
They focus excessive attention on me,
While I much prefer that they just let me be.

Joann Sprangers Lee

New York Women

The women of this city love to dress in muted tones,
In subtle shades of black and white and beige and brown and bones.
In every New York office classy ladies look like wrens,
As dull and unobtrusive as a flock of sparrow hens.
The skirts are black, the tops are beige, tomorrow the reverse,
As though all color were sucked out by monotoning curse.
I moved here as a parrot and it took me many years
To move from red to brown and gray, to shift my color gears,
To mute my rainbow wardrobe from the colorful Midwest,
And look as brown and beige and gray in New York as the rest.
Yet in my heart I'm still a parrot here among the wrens,
And long to see the parrots soar beyond the gray bird trends.
But fear of such a bold attempt has kept me dressed in gray,
And kept my bright red linen pants still safely tucked away.

Opportunity

Opportunity knocked and I opened the door
And thought I had seen that old geezer before.
A chance I'd rejected had rolled by again.
Instead of accepting I just asked him when
He might come back knocking once more on my door.
He shook his head sadly and said "nevermore."

No Pets, Please

It's hard for cats to understand
Why I do not extend my hand
To pat their heads or pet their fur
In answer to a friendly purr.
Long years ago at Mother's knee
The lesson that was taught to me
Was "wash your hands if you touch that
Old germy dog or germy cat."
It's etched so deeply in my brain
That I will grumble and complain
If friendly pets hop on my knee
And spread their germs all over me.
My friend's black Lab smells like a sewer
So weekend visits are now fewer.
I'd keep the bedroom door tight shut
To keep out germs and smelly mutt.
Right after a quick pee one night
There on the bed an awful sight.
Plopped on my pillow black Lab head,
His big black butt wiped on the bed.
Oh yikes and horrors—hairy bed.
A trillion germs. I'll soon be dead.
Forgive me should you notice that
I'm disinclined to pet your cat.

November Wedding

To wed in November can come with great cost.
Your guests will most likely be sprinkled with frost.
The soft summer dresses have been packed away.
It's goose bumps and flannel for your wedding day.
No garlands of daisies on bride Kelsey's head.
They're now out-of-season—all dried up and dead.
What still is in season with autumn just past?
Perhaps a few pumpkins that managed to last.
There's small competition for church or for hall,
But lots of dried cornstalks to lean on the wall.
A bride in white flannel with wee bits of lace
Could set the right tone and seem really in place.
A veil trimmed in down would be so apropos
And match the white cashmere tuxedo for Joe.
Carry the flowers with fur-lined white glove
And live your whole lives filled with warmth and with love.

Onion

Onion, onion pointed and green,
Pure white ball with silky sheen.
What a delicate sweet design.
Yet you bite this tongue of mine.

Org of the Orchard

My brother Org has apple trees.
He started with a few.
With fertile land and fertile mind
The trees and orchard grew.
And every year you could drive by
And see that more and more
Have joined the many hundreds that
Were growing there before.
He bought more land; he bought more trees.
We thought he'd never stop.
But then we got to wondering
Who really is on top?
"Does he own trees or they own him?"
We shake our heads and say.
While trees just laze around the field,
He works for them all day.

Pen Points

Fat pens are too noisy and shout out their words
Demanding attention and that they be heard.
My favorite pen has a point that is thin
To very concisely express what's within.

Joann Sprangers Lee

Out of Biz

I passed a closing shop today.
A sign hung on the door,
"Very soon we're sad to say
You will not see our store.
We gladly served our neighbors here
For forty years or so.
Our lease ran out, can't be renewed.
So now we're forced to go."
I'd never shopped in that small store
And seldom pass this way.
But felt some sadness nonetheless
To see its dying day.

Party Pooper

I dread being part of a crowd
No matter the size, it's too loud.
At picnic or party or wedding
It's making that small talk I'm dreading.
As much as I'd like to be there,
With good food and booze we could share,
There is someplace else I must be
That has a soft chair and TV.

Packing Light

I'm trying hard at packing light
But in the middle of the night
A lot of clothes I will not wear
Sneak quietly from who knows where
And hide themselves in my suitcase—
The biggest one with lots of space.
So every day I must unpack
And every night they all sneak back.
I fear it is a losing fight.
I now give up. I can't pack light.
So when you see me at your door
Don't ask what all those clothes are for.
They smuggled themselves all inside,
Not to be worn, but for the ride.

Patience

When God was handing patience out I would not wait in line.
The process was too tedious. I don't like wasting time.
I now wish that I had some patience as through life I go
Always stuck behind someone who's moving way too slow.

Joann Sprangers Lee

Perfect Place to Work

They all look picture perfect
And they all have perfect lives.
The men make perfect husbands
And the women perfect wives.
Their children are all perfect
And get smarter every year.
They all make perfect money
In a well-defined career.
But something seems to happen
When they reach a certain year.
Sometime before they're fifty
They seem to disappear.

Story Telling

Dearest friend, I beg you not
Bore me with that detailed plot
Of the latest book that you just read.
Unfortunately your retelling
Of the plot is not compelling
Or you would have written it instead.

Playwright's Lament

There are a million plays out there
That really should have gone somewhere.
The plots are clever, brilliant, witty.
All have flopped; oh what a pity.
Failure is a crying shame
And actors are the ones to blame.

They are essential I'll admit.
Without them there's no living script.
Some mumble where loud rants should be.
Some yell out every subtlety.
Who ripped to shreds the playwright's name?
Those actors are the ones I blame.

My play was written, oh, so well.
Suspense was building; I could tell.
Who spoke too loud, too fast, too slow?
Who dealt my masterpiece a blow?
Who killed my chances at great fame?
The actors must take all the blame.

I'm destined for the Great White Way.
My name in lights? Yes, any day.
But there has been a slight delay
Based on what critics have to say.
They said my play is trite and lame.
But I say actors are to blame.
Those actors are the ones to blame.

Potty Pose

When I would take a bathroom break
A certain effort it would take
To make it without accident.
I walked with my back slightly bent
To keep from dampening my clothes.
My son would yell out "potty pose."
As many years now trickle by
I sadly find that often I
Run office halls with back that's bent
To stop that same old accident.
And always fear my posture shows
That I am in a potty pose.

Rainy Day

I love brand new rain and its watery smell
It seems to portend that things soon will be well.
The grasses made sparkling and glistening by
A sprinkling can tipped through the clouds in the sky.

Priorities

The list of my priorities through years remains unchanged
Although a couple items have been slightly rearranged.
A sense of humor always was and still is at the top,
And somewhere in the middle is "I love to bargain shop."
Squarely on the little list, "Be pleasant and be kind;
Then always be inquisitive and keep an open mind."
Oh, what's that on the bottom, hiding way down on the sheet?
A little smudged and blurry "Keep my house real clean and neat."

Reincarnation

Reincarnation? I believe it is true.
And each time you leave I mourn and miss you.
This old repetition is getting so dreary.
Next time we are parted, let's try to be cheery,
Knowing we'll soon be together again,
And that the next meeting is just round the bend.

Reconfiguration

My new cube is cozy, my new cube is small.
When I roll back quickly, my head hits the wall

Joann Sprangers Lee

Rabbit Rides

They're breeding like rabbits in city and town
And munching the tree bark and flower stems down.
Pressure is mounting that we get along.
(Nadine, for one, thinks to kill them is wrong.)
I think there's a way we can solve this great threat
Without your retaining those rabbits as pets.
Humanely displace them by setting a trap,
Then move them all to a new spot on the map.
Each night after supper you must take a drive
To move today's rabbit that you've trapped alive.
The rabbits will start to appreciate you
And that nightly effort to alter their view.
From city to country again and again.
In their little apple and carrot filled pen.
Each night human trappers will drive out of town
To free today's rabbit to new munching ground.
The rabbits will love all this traveling too
And try very hard to run right back to you.

Read a Book

I take a book,
Give one quick look
By scanning just page one.
So fast I feel
There's no appeal.
To read this is no fun.
This book's been tried
Now cast aside
Without a second look.
Perhaps I ought
To give more thought
To reading one whole book.
To speed-dismiss
All books like this,
My judgment is askew.
I now declare
I'll be more fair
And also read page two.

Retiring

We'd like to thank young folks out there
For showing us how much you care.
We know you have to scrimp and scrounge
So we can all retire and lounge.
Yup, we retire at sixty-two,
But must depend on dough from you.
Yet sad to say too bad for you,
You'll not retire at sixty-two,
For all the money will be spent,
And we'll be too dead to repent.
So in the meantime work real hard.
We're in the hammock in the yard.

Rhyme Time

Like sands start slow
Then faster go
The longer that you pour.
The more I rhyme
The less the time
It takes to rhyme some more.

Ron S(hhh)

I have a quiet brother who does not have much to say.
He goes about his business very quietly each day.
When he's attacked he will not fight, but slowly slips away
And thinks that putting up a fight is not the RS way.
He has that shy recessive gene that dots our family
To add some quiet subtlety when things go rowdily.
So how extraordinarily wise that he should choose to mate
With someone who can take the bat and move up to the plate
And hit each ball that whizzes by her head or that of Ron,
Protecting Ronny's quiet self when trouble's coming on.
He stands aside and smiles as Cindy jumps into the fray
And grins as she plows to the side the problems of the day.

Senator

Find a senator just like me
A bit tight-fisted—miserly,
Who watches every cent he spends
And knows my take-home pay depends
On thrift he shows down in DC.
To do it right, please vote for me!

Sugared

Drink eight glasses every day.
Water is the best.
Cleans the sludge out of the bod.
Helps your system rest.

Ron likes sugar, Ron likes taste.
Water is no fun.
Forty-thousand Pepsi cans
Emptied one by one.

Just like Annabel before,
Pepsi is his drink.
Nothing crystal clear for health,
He thinks that water stinks.

When they do a blood test now
To see if it caused harm,
Veins are full of Pepsi please
Flowing through his arm.

Sugar high and sugar low
May have zapped The Ron,
Knocked him out some months ago
Standing in the john.

All's not lost, there is still time
To turn his life around.
Turn the Pepsi spigot off
And lose a hundred pounds.

Watch him exercise each day,
Walk five miles is best.
Change his diet drastically
Or it's eternal rest.

James T of the North Woods

I have a brother who loves wood.
He owns a forest, so he should.
He has a CAT to knock trees down
And plow some roads to get around.
He taps the maples, and what's more
His sawmill hugs the forest floor.
He built a chapel all of wood
From crafty logs built where they stood
To greet God in a woodsy way,
A place wood lovers love to pray.

Rubber Boots

My waterproof boots reach right up to my knees
And keep out the snow, so my feet do not freeze.
I walk through deep puddles and never get wet
From water outside, but inside feet sweat.

Seventy-Five

I'm seventy-five, alive and well
Though in decline as you can tell.
My hair is thin while I am not.
My once flat stomach has a pot.
My spine was straight but now is bent.
All my youth has now been spent.
In light of what you have just read,
I'm seventy-five and nearly dead.

Shade

I hate bright sunshine in my eye
So do my best (at least I try)
To stand in some cool shady spot
To wait for buses when it's hot.
Alas, the bus stop I use most
Has not a tree, just one lamp post.
I try aligning head and eyes
In what slim shade the post provides.
The shadow of us both combined,
Though lamp-post shaped, has my behind.

Shaky Seattle

Steph lives in Seattle where the city had the shakes.
Psychics long predicted it would have some bad earthquakes.
Nervous buildings shedded bricks that smacked the shaking ground.
Printers moved across the floor and chased the staff around.
So much china, so much glass in pieces on the floor.
Big decision: run outside or stand inside the door?
Looked as though a bomb had dropped, the city was at war.
This was a little quake, but don't you wonder what's in store?
Will the city next time shake into the nearby sea?
Is it time to move inland or will you wait and see?

Shoe Search

A birthday party? Where are my best shoes?
A single left shoe is a strange thing to lose.
The little shoe mountain on my closet floor
Holds old shoes and new shoes and shoes, shoes galore.
I sent the shoes airborne to find my lost shoe.
Where could it be hiding? I don't have a clue.
The baffling dilemma of that one lost shoe
Is solved if I hop. So that's what I will do.

Silver Suit

Her shiny silver pants suit was not easy to ignore.
Was granny heading off to some unusual clothing store?
With neatly tied black sneakers on her going-somewhere feet,
She's not the usual office worker on the morning street.
Too late to be returning from a night out on-the-town,
Although her makeup and red hair look like she gets around.
Her shopping bag was gold Godiva and was giant size.
Godiva's half-pound chocolates are not the one's she buys.
She hurried off the bus like someone with no time to spare.
A destination on Sixth Avenue? I wonder where.
Could she be working at a job she started long ago
Where she has worked and watched three generations come and go?
Perhaps they try to humor her as she still works away
And pounds a little keyboard year-by-year and day-by-day.
Each office needs a granny with the same eccentric flair.
I wonder if I can pick up a silver suit somewhere.

Scotch Tape

Little piece of Scotch tape
Repaired my ripped up line,
Took the sentence I destroyed
And made it sound just fine.

Small Talk

I dislike petty small talk like, "How is the weather there?"
"And how was your vacation?" as though I really care.
So should I meet you on the street, you'll never hear me say
Such meaningless and trite a greeting as, "How are you today?"
I find it much more meaningful to take a larger view
And ask with calculating stare, has life been good to you?
Do you believe in aliens or that you've lived before?
Please rate your marriage one to ten and is your mate a bore?
What is your prime philosophy and do you often pray?
What is the status of your soul? What's in your DNA?
Do you believe in destiny, that it might be revealed
That long before you came to earth your fate had all been sealed?
Why, yes, I'd love to spend the weekend. Tell me what to wear.
So how was your vacation? And how's the weather there?"

Shopping

I'm watching her size
And things that she buys
In Saturday's grocery line.
When she buys French fries
It shows in her size,
But please keep your eyes off of mine.

Smokes

Small clusters of addicts chitchat on the street
With bunches of bent butts surrounding their feet,
Exhaling smoke signals that rise overhead
Announcing indifference to what lies ahead:
The coughing when lungs reach a coal shade of black,
The sallow skin tones caused by oxygen's lack.
It's inhale and exhale the poison they choose.
It's suicide slowly, but there is good news.
When comes the day they have coughed their last cough,
Attending a funeral means a day off.

Sonia

Sonia wears round glasses with a Harry Potter flair.
Sonia's pitch black wizard glasses match her pitch black hair.
Sonia's life is pleasant, as it has been for a while.
Sonia's very happy with a friendly laugh and smile.
Sonia had a lot of boy friends that she casts aside.
Sonia is too clever to become a ho-hum bride.
Sonia is a lawyer and she is too smart for that.
Sonia like all wizards thinks that she can smell a rat.
Sonia does not want to live beneath some husband's thumb.
Sonia, move with caution. Wizards sometimes marry bums.

Snow Flake

The first flake of a snowy storm tapped gently on my arm,
To warn me that a storm approached and that it meant no harm.
Like first note of an opera, you know there's more to come,
That they will build upon themselves with drifts and strings and drums.
I'd like to thank that little flake for warning what's in store,
But cannot find my snowy friend among the trillions more.

Snow Predicted

Snow is predicted, so I dressed up today
In boots and warm coat and my mittens to play.
But this is the city where snow does not stick
But makes the streets slushy and mushy and slick.
I want winter fields that I walked long ago
With hoof prints of deer on the trails in the snow,
And every direction a Christmas card scene
With big clumps of snow plopped on each evergreen,
And sparkling ice crystals on branches of trees,
Like fairytale woods, will we get some of these?
Or must I just hope that the snow will soon stop
And not once again fill the city with slop?

So Long, Friend

The reason we are friends is that you're traveling my way.
Our lives are somehow parallel at church or work or play.
I did not do a massive search or even interview,
But one day with no special effort found a friend in you.
It is a wondrous thing how we can find some soul out there
To meet and greet and talk and laugh and find we really care.
So we will lunch and share our lives and share our worries, too.
We will provide each other shoulders; we will be true blue.
But just as baffling as a friendship's most auspicious start
Is that one day when paths diverge we'll slowly drift apart.
For interest often wanes when friends are slightly out-of-view,
So if you move, please don't expect me to remember you.

Spidery Spin

I saw a spider on the wall
Just as it was about to fall.
It caught itself with string of spit
And wove a dainty web with it.

Swim

I'd swim if there would be a way
To hold my head above the fray.
I'd like to do long laps and yet
I do not want my head all wet.

Spring Ends

I walked down the street
In too much April heat
A rainstorm of petals pinked sidewalk concrete.
The drops looked so sweet
As they fell to the street
But soon were destroyed by the stomping of feet.

Spring Fever

I have a touch of spring malaise
That comes upon me warm spring days.
It gives my energy a zap.
Excuse me. Time to take a nap.

Spring Heat Wave

I fondly remember last winter.
We had just one teeny cold spell.
As winters go, it was a sissy.
I hate cold, so thought it was swell.
Now weather has changed with a vengeance.
It's April and hotter than hell.

Stephanie is Baking

Stephanie just emailed me a list of her desserts,
Then casually included news she cannot close her skirts.
Oh Stephanie, dear Stephanie, I've been through this before.
That pound attained with sweets is gained and with you evermore.
The rhubarb crisp may taste divine as does the chocolate cake,
But yummy sweets and fresh baked treats are all that it will take
To plump you up sweet ounce-by-ounce a little every year
Until like all the rest of us you have a big fat rear.

Strategy

I know not the manner by which I'll survive.
I know not the strategy to stay alive.
I know not the trick to avoid heart attacks.
I hope it does not it mean I must give up snacks.

Stringy Bean

I do not know where I have seen
A slender, tender, greener bean.
Keep growing for a bigger treat!
Oh, oh! You're now too tough to eat.

Stockings

When I was four or maybe five.
Our mother's dresser drawer
Was filled with twisted stockings
Overflowing to the floor.

It was a jumble jangle of
A hundred different hues,
Unsorted, stuffed together, so
She didn't know which to use.

Wash them, stuff them in the drawer,
When it is time to dress,
Open a new package, and
I do that, I confess.

Could this be one more curse of genes
That has me do the same?
My drawer of twisted knee hi's,
Is Annabel to blame?

Temperatures Rising

When I was young we sweltered in the heat without AC.
But way back then the heat did not seem quite so hot to me.

Sunrise

I've always hated sunrise.
It's too bright much too soon.
How much more I would love it
If it would rise at noon.

Sunset

I patiently watched for the sun to slip down
And paint red and purple the skies of the town.
The sun in a bad mood left skies bleak and gray.
The old party pooper did not want to play.

Summer Linen

A lady dressed in summer linen is a wrinkled mess.
Her shirts and skirts and dresses all could use a good hot press.
But when the cooler breeze foretells that autumn will begin,
She puts her wrinkled clothes away and looks neat as a pin.

Weight Lost

In the mirror every morn I see I've lost a pound.
Every evening it comes back and I'm still fat and round.

Sweets Murder

Who's trying to kill him with fat?
Could someone be plotting like that?
To get all of his apple trees?
To cash in those life policies?
And how will they murder the man?
A sweets and a chocolate plan.
Addicted to ice cream and sweets,
Whatever he sees, yes, he eats.
Fill up the house up with ice cream.
A natural death it will seem.
And no one will know at the time.
It has been a sweet perfect crime.

Taxing

The tax man is coming, he's coming today
To take along with him the bulk of your pay.
You chose to ignore there's a big balance due.
The tax man is mean and he's gunning for you.
You closed your eyes tight and hoped he'd go away.
That trick did not work, so bye-bye to your pay.

Taylor

I saw her on the busy street. She had a bright tattoo
With her name "Taylor" on her arm in green and red and blue,
And peaking from her scarlet shoes, a toe with silver ring.
She had the flair and attitude that confidence can bring.
Dark ringlets fell way down her back. She had a take-charge stride.
I'll bet there are a hundred men who want her as their bride.
You surely are quite popular, Ms. Taylor from the street.
I saw the glances you receive from everyone you meet.
I did not even see your face, but I admire you,
And wish that I at 21 would have been a Taylor, too.
But I was just the opposite, quite frumpy I admit,
Without your little scarlet skirt, that tight but perfect fit.
Perhaps I took the wrong approach and kept my light too dim.
I should have jumped in with both feet and had a rousing swim.
I wonder what life could have been, or would it be the same,
With silver ring upon my toe and Taylor as my name.

Trees

I love to stand beneath a tree and look up to the sky
And watch the leaves and branches wave as birds go gliding by.
It is so strong and sturdy, but so filled with humor too.
It holds a steady perch for birds to sit and poop on you.

Teapot from Pike's Market

Its shape a yellow lemon; my teapot looks so bright.
Although it is good looking, it does not pour tea right.
The green spout's poorly engineered, so tea spills everywhere –
On tablecloth and table, on visitor and chair.
I'd love to use that teapot but tea time is no fun.
That teapot is a lemon in lot more ways than one.

Thinking Out Loud

If all our thoughts were heard out loud, oh what a sorry day.
Please move it faster, tubby, your butt is in my way.
Your dress is dirty, grandma, with spots all down the side.
Why did you date that loud-mouthed girl and take her as your bride?
Your home looks awfully beige to me, so tasteless, bland and grim.
Your husband's stupid and a bore. Why did you marry him?
You never cease your talking. Please stop and take a breath?
That endless mindless chatter of yours bores me half to death.
You paid how much for that new suit that does not fit you well?
The gray is showing in your hair, besides you look like hell.
Of course, I do not think such things nor would I all the while
Our paths are crossing on the street as I say "hi" and smile.

When I Was Thin

When I was young and thin as you,
Quite honestly good looking too,
I in the future did not see
That someday I would look like me.

Thrift Shop Apron

I thank you for the apron that you sewed with such great care.
I thank you, Sister Stephanie, it's one I always wear.
I bought it in a thrift shop in your small Wisconsin town.
Your old pink convent apron has picked up and moved around.
Though three of us were from small towns, two of us left somehow
To make a new home in New York where we're both living now.
Your nametag is still fastened with your crooked little stitch.
The ties in back are somewhat high and close to my armpits.
I think your apron's happy with the strange new path it took.
It seems to love it in New York and really likes to cook.

Unrequited

If ever I should see once more
The man that I so loved before
I hope he's struck with sharp regret
That he dismissed my love, and yet
The greater thrill for me would be
To then dump him as he did me.

Voice

My sister chose an angel's voice when it was choosing time.
I chose instead the talent to concoct a clever rhyme.
But when I hear the choir sing, I second-guess my choice,
And wish that God had added to my rhymes a pretty voice.

Trike Attack

At four I drove my new red trike
Into someone I did not like.
Though usually not a violent child
Old grandma's wrinkles somehow riled
Up my dislike of ugliness.
I tried to wipe out that old mess.
Alas, revenge of life draws near.
Now when I glance into a mirror
I see a face some kid won't like
And fear attack by evil trike.

Turtle Walk

By what bizarre, perverse design
Are pokies always first in line.
They block the sidewalks when they walk
And dilly-dally while they talk.
It's not as irksome I have found
Where there is room to zoom around.
But as a general rule I'd say
Too often snails are in my way.
I am impatient. I move fast.
You turtle butts, please let me past.

Umbrella Shared

Forgot your umbrella?
Oh, what a great shame!
You seem to think I should
Accept half the blame.
You did the forgetting.
If I share it's true
That I will be half dry
And half wet like you.

Violet Shy

The violet and the buttercup
Were rather scarce when I grew up
And prized much more for scarcity
Just as less talk from you would be.

Volunteer Anyone?

Volunteering is the way
That you work hard for zero pay.
Benefits of this pay rate?
You can't buy food, so you'll lose weight.
Others with less work to do
Will not get paid lot more than you.
You'll then avoid those painful days
You would spend begging for a raise.

Walk in the City

When living in this city you will find you walk each day.
A car is never parked outside to whisk you on your way.
Instead you use left, right, left, right to get you here and there,
Especially when it's nice out and you have the time to spare.
So city residents are often much more firmly fit
Than couch potatoes who will drive and are inclined to sit.
The worst thing about living here and walking all around
(And much to my dismay it happens often, I have found)
You're halfway where you want to be or almost halfway back.
That's when you feel it coming on—the dreaded poop attack!
There is no bathroom that you know along this avenue.
Do you walk faster or slow down? I'll leave that up to you.

Waterproofed

My coat and hat, black vinyl, in the closet wait for rain
And plan to keep me dry when drops beat on the windowpane.
The southeast storm blows in with torrents whistling all around,
Spinning horizontally and spitting on the ground.
There is no need for me to cower underneath some roof.
Out in the storm I bravely stride because I'm waterproof.

Joann Sprangers Lee

What an Old Lady Wears

Nobody cares
What an old lady wears
Except the old lady herself.
Her favorite designers,
No longer headliners,
Are old hat like hats on her shelf.
That dress from the fifties
Still looks mighty nifty
She thinks as she strikes her old pose.
And that is the reason
Why every new season
She claims she does not need new clothes

When I Was Young

When I was young and five-foot-ten
I was much taller than most men.
Old age produced a shorter me.
I'm five-foot-eight, but woe is me.
Those cute guys shrunk to five-foot-seven,
Or even worse, they went to heaven.

Which Way?

My sense of direction I'm sorry to say
Is constantly sending me off the wrong way.
If I am to get there while it is still light,
I'll have to turn left though I feel right is right.

Wild Apples

Ever see an apple tree
Growing wild and growing free?
Lovely blossoms in the spring,
But the crop that fall will bring –
Crippled, gnarly, wormy fruit,
And a sour taste to boot.
It's a mighty price to pay –
Apples Mother Nature's way.

Window West

I was born at set of sun
And love to see it set.
Fate is cruel, I've not had
A western window yet.

Joann Sprangers Lee

Spain and France and Italy

Spain and France and Italy.
The tour was great. What did I see?
Um, sad to say I can't recall.
I do believe we had ball.
The food was great or good or fair.
I ate it all, so must not care.
The people on the bus were swell,
All crammed together you can tell
Nice folks don't crab and make a fuss
When squished for hours on a bus.
I have great photos of the trip,
But here is where I made a slip.
I wonder where those sights might be—
Spain or France or Italy?

Thank$

It's nice to be appreciated
Even when you're overrated.
For the cash and card, I give my thanks.
Flowers tend to wilt and die
While candy sends blood sugar high,
But cash is welcome at all stores and banks.

Words Anyone?

How many words fit in your brain
Without it bursting from the strain?
I know people now attending
Meetings, meetings without ending.
Seven hours every day.
Who could have that much to say?
Facts and figures, theories, quotes,
Decks of Powerpoint with notes.
Hundred-fifty words per minute.
Does your brain have any limit?
Words to hear and words to say.
Sixty-thousand words per day
Squeezed in tight where they remain
Crowding neurons in your brain.
Are you working at retaining
What small brain space you've remaining?
There's a meeting? Should you go?
Will it be the final blow?
Will your brain explode? Who knows?
Spilling words mess up your clothes.

Joann Sprangers Lee

Woman in Red

Woman in Red along the wall
Of staid accounting company's hall.
You seem a bit incongruous
With red silk, off-the-shoulder dress
And skirt that's flying in the air
To almost show your underwear.
Because I sat across the way
I heard the comments every day.
You got a glance and maybe sneer
As they asked, "How did she get here?"
You're most outrageous of them all—
The movie posters on the wall.
How clever of you to slip in
To hallowed halls with hint of sin.

Waiting Room

I'm waiting for the doctor.
What a splendid chance for me
To wile all the hours away—
As opportunity
To do some writing. After all
I came here close to noon.
The notebook slowly filling up
Will be a novel soon.

Apple Tree Pruner

The apple tree pruner is flopping around
And spending too much time prostrate on the ground.
He's spinning and falling and plunging from trees
Down into the snow drifts with buckling knees.
He tries pruning trees but they give him a whack
And watch as he flips down and falls on his back.
He's saved from a splat by a huge bank of snow
That cushions old Rogie and eases the blow.
What will become of him when soon melts the snow
And there's no soft cushion to catch him below.
Expense will be mighty if now we must plan
To make snow all summer to catch pruning man.

Water a Melon

Watermelon, red and juicy and impressive size
On a skinny stem and what nutrition it supplies.
Mystery of nature how it gets so fat and round
From anything that stem sucks out of the dirty ground.

Ginny & Herb

Ginny and Herb in the state of "LA".
Ginny and Herb are not working today.
It's through absolutely no fault of their own.
That they're unemployed and both sitting at home.
One had a bad boss and the other bad back.
Herb is disabled and Gin got the sack.
Their minds scheme and plan for a much richer day.
A doggie motel is an excellent way.
But they need some cash to get started they say.
If your dog has spare cash, would he send it their way
To impress his dog friends when they hear him tell
That he is part owner of a doggie motel?

Walk and Talk

It is a balmy night
For us to take a walk.
It is a starry night.
For us to stroll and talk.
A friend on nights like this
I so appreciate.
It's all your boring stories
That make me so irate.

When Death Comes to Call

She accepted the bad news with guts, said, "Okay,
I think I will throw a nice party one day,"
Where she would invite all the good friends she knew
They'd stop by to chat and perhaps have a few.
Instead of a funeral after she died
She said, "Throw a party" through tears, yes she cried.
But when came the time she did not want to go.
Agreeing at first but then said, "No no no."
She'd say, "I feel worse, but how can this be?"
And mentioned the subject of death seldomly.
It pains me to see how you're fighting for breath
And struggling daily to ward off your death.
I wish you the best in this fight, my dear friend.
But, alas, death holds all of the cards at the end.
You did a great job and you played your life well.
Much of it I know from the stories you tell.
You don't want your play cut off so soon, I know.
You want lot more time and I pray it is so,
But only death knows when it closes the show.

Torch

Rejected in his twenties,
He wishes fate were kind.
His life would be so different
If she had changed her mind.

In dead of night and dead of sleep
He knows not where or when,
She'll visit in his dreams at night,
Elusive now as then.

He sees her in his mind's eye
As always young and fair.
Because he has not watched her age –
Get wrinkles and gray hair

Our hearts play crazy tricks on us –
That sweet girl blonde & fair
May now be just a wrinkled hag
With head of Brillo hair.

Me, Myself or I?

(A grammar lesson for co-workers)

It will be a confirmation
Of your grammar limitation
If you use "myself" or "I" in place of "me."

I will give a brief example
That with luck you should find ample.
To discern what proper use should be.

If I ask you out tonight
With friends and "me" I've done it right.
With friends and "I" or "myself" is a grammar wrong.

If you're put in that position
(Object of a preposition)
Means you really must take "me" along.

Connie to Wed

If you judge a workload by the time one has to chat,
Connie works the hardest; we'll all agree with that.
While others on the team are lunching, Connie taps her keys
And analyzes, calculates, and swears in Cantonese.
Many that preceded her have buckled from the strain,
Because they did not have her toughness or her speedy brain.
But this may not be such good news for Van in their new life,
Because she won't have time to clean or be a cooking wife.
While Van is in the kitchen slicing, cooking, stirring, chopping,
Connie, working day and night, continues her laptopping.
In spite of this, we wish them well and know things will work right,
Because if nothing else she'll never have the time to fight.

Wish to Fish

If I would have a boat to fish,
It would fulfill my fondest wish
To take the time I want to take,
To live life simply on a lake—
Deep in the woods, trees all around,
The sounds of nature, so profound.
Or would I then get bored and aim
For city life from which I came?

Mighty Munching Man

Let's watch mighty munching man
Toss in food with hefty hand.
Special love of Hershey kisses
Perfect aim, he never misses.
Watch both hands unwrap and eat,
Wrappers pile up at his feet.
What new goodies might he like?
Ice cream bars, he'll have Klondike.
Bowl of ice cream topped with what's
Maple syrup and hickory nuts.
How he savors every taste.
How it blows up Rogie's waist.

Sara Bean

Sara has a garden and it covers half the lot.
Sara wanted string beans and that is what she's got.
String beans growing, string beans bagged and string beans everywhere.
Sara over-beaned one time but now plants beans with care.

Joann Sprangers Lee

Small Town Girl

In the town where I was born
Daily strolls meant seeing these:
Oak and elm and ash and maple,
Lots of grass and lots of trees.
Thought I'd visit someplace larger—
To New York to look around,
Where the strolls are never boring –
Lots of sights and lots of sound,
Shops with food and shops with trinkets,
Shops with burgers, donuts, cash,
Lots of different kinds of people,
Lots of banks and lots of trash.
Once a year I visit Darboy
For a peek at greenery.
But my heart's stuck in the city
Filled with all there is to see.
Careful where you choose to visit
When you feel the urge to roam.
That huge crowded, crazy city
May become your brand new home.

Andrea

Andrea's a microchip
She thinks and talks fast as a whip.
A bit impatient as you know,
Completes your sentence if you're slow.
Keep it pithy, move along
Or when you finish, she'll be gone.
Though she's brilliant and upbeat,
She has one failing; it's "delete".
On a slow December day
This failing carried her away.
To make her calendar look neat
She thought "What fun if I delete"
All the meetings, one Town Hall.
Waste of time. Delete them all.
Team meetings move a bit too slow.
And they're boring. Off they go.
Nothing much she tried to save.
Delete updates with her boss Dave.
In December if she's in
Her cubicle with that sly grin.
Take a little tip from me
You'd best delete her delete key.

Joann Sprangers Lee

And Now For The Song Section.

Or shall we say the hymn section. On the next page is the hymn I wrote and could never get a choir to take seriously. I want to see it in print so why not include it in my book of rhymes. After all, the lines of the hymn do rhyme.

With a Twist of Rhyme

Lay Your Healing Hands on Me

Joann Sprangers Lee ©2001

I'm be-set by trials and trou-bles. I'm in mis-er-
When the sun is cov-ered o-ver and my world seems
In this world you see your peo-ple hate and fight and
When I'm filled with black des-pair and life's tra-vails have

-y and pain. Lord ex-tend your hand to heal me
dark and gray. When you see your child-ren strug-gle,
go to war. Please shine down your lov-ing kind-ness
swamped my soul. Pick me up from dark-ened tren-ches;

and to make me whole a-gain. When I walk those
bright-en up our drear-y day. Ill-ness-es of
so our hearts will hate no more. Save me from all
make my heart and spir-it whole. Show-er me with

deep dark val-leys that are strewn a-long my way.
mind and spir-it, ill-ness-es of bod-y, soul.
life's mis-for-tune, heal my heart of all its pain.
light and beau-ty, like a flow-er in the sun.

Copyright ©2001 by Joann Sprangers Lee
All Rights Reserved

Joann Sprangers Lee